Pebble® Plus

Spokes

SIMPLE BIKE MAINTENANCE
Time for a Tune-Up!
BY LISA J. AMSTUTZ

raintree

a Capstone company — publishers for children

Raintree is an imprint of Capstone Global Library Limited, a company incorporated in England and Wales having its registered office at 264 Banbury Road, Oxford, OX2 7DY – Registered company number: 6695582

www.raintree.co.uk
myorders@raintree.co.uk

Edited by Jeni Wittrock
Designed by Kyle Grenz
Production by Jennifer Walker
Picture research by Sarah Schuette
Photo Schedule by Marcy Morin
Production by Capstone Global Library Ltd
Printed and bound in China

ISBN 978 1 4747 3371 7
20 19 18 17 16
10 9 8 7 6 5 4 3 2 1

British Library Cataloguing in Publication Data
A full catalogue record for this book is available from the British Library.

Acknowledgements
We would like to thank the following for permission to reproduce photographs: Alamy: Alvey & Towers Picture Library, 13; BananaStock, Ltd., 17; Capstone Studio: Karon Dubke, 9, 15, 19; Getty Images: The Image Bank/Ariel Skelley, 5; iStockphotos: BartCo, 21, Ed Hidden, 7, ktmoffitt, 11; Shutterstock: Sergiy Zavgorodny, cover

Design Elements
Shutterstock: filip robert, Kalmatsuy Tatyana

We would like to thank Gail Saunders-Smith for her invaluable help in the preparation of this book.

Contents

Bikes need care

A bike takes you where you need to go. But a rusty or broken bike is hard to use. Take care of your bike so you're always ready to ride.

5

Before you ride

Full tyres keep your bike rolling.

Tyres should feel firm. If not,

an adult can help you add air.

Use a tyre pump to fill the tyres.

Look carefully at the
grooves in the tyres.
Remove any chunks of dirt
or rocks from the tread.
Check for cuts or holes.

tyre treads

Safety check

Loose bike parts are unsafe.

Hold the front wheel steady.

Try to turn the handlebars.

If they wiggle, tighten them.

The seat should be tight too.

Does your bike have hand
brakes? Roll the bike forward
and squeeze one brake.
The bike should stop quickly.
Now test the other brake.

hand brake

After you ride

Clean a dirty bike with water and soap. Rinse and dry it well. Park your bike indoors or cover it. Wet bikes rust!

After washing your bike,

lube the chain to prevent rust.

Add chain oil as you turn

the pedals backwards.

Wipe off drips with a rag.

Tune-up time

Once or twice a year, give
the bike a full wash and wax.
Degrease the chain and wipe
it clean. Then lube it again.

Once a year take your bike
to a bike shop. Let a pro give
your bike a full check-up.
A little extra care will keep
you pedalling safely!

Glossary

chain oil type of oil used on bike chains; chain oil keeps bike gears and chains running smoothly

degrease remove grease or oil using a special cleaner

lube apply oil or grease

maintain keep in good shape

rust become covered in a reddish brown substance; rust forms when iron or steel stays wet

tread series of bumps and grooves on a tyre

tyre pump tool used for adding air to a tyre

wax put wax or polish on something; wax keeps bikes from rusting

Read more

Bicycles (Made by Hand), Patricia Larkin (Aladdin, 2017)

Bike: In 10 Simple Steps (How to Design the World's Best), Paul Mason (Wayland, 2016)

Mountain Biking (Exploring the Outdoors), Michael De Medeiros (AV2, 2013)

Websites

news.bbc.co.uk/sport2/hi/other_sports/cycling/get_involved/4250522.stm
Learn about bike maintenance from this BBC website.

www.sustrans.org.uk/what-you-can-do/cycling/your-bike/bicycle-maintenance-made-easy
Maintain and repair your bike with these helpful tips and guides.

Index